# Running Rugby

# RUNNING RUGBY

Ray French

Foreword by Des Seabrook
Preface by Mike Davis

*Line Drawings by Ken Tranter*

**Faber and Faber**
London   Boston

*First published in 1980*
*by Faber and Faber Limited*
*3 Queen Square London WC1N 3AU*
*Printed in Great Britain by*
*Fakenham Press Limited, Fakenham, Norfolk*
*All rights reserved*

© *Ray French 1980*

*British Library Cataloguing in Publication Data*

*French, Ray*
  *Running rugby.*
  *1. Rugby football coaching*
  *I. Title*
  *796.33'3'077      GV945.75*

  *ISBN 0–571–11597–7*
  *ISBN 0–571–11600–0 Pbk*

# Contents

# List of Illustrations

# Foreword

Having been an advocate of attacking, adventurous rugby, I am delighted to write a foreword for Ray's book. His approach to the game has been an example to everybody in it.

If we were to trace the rugby pedigree of many of our senior internationals, we would find that they attended traditional rugby schools where they mastered many of the game's basic skills.

Playing against, and watching, Cowley School over the last twenty years have left a conviction that their adventurous approach, coupled with their command of the basic handling skills, is a model for all schoolboys to follow. They are encouraged to handle and run with the ball, and to me that is the essence of rugby. As John Burgess has truly said, 'exciting and exhilarating rugby is the result of doing simple things well.'

In this book Ray shares the knowledge and expertise he has acquired over the years as a player and coach. Its message is one that should fire the imagination of all those involved in the game at this level—a bible for the future well-being of our game.

DES SEABROOK
*Coach, Orrell R.F.C. and Lancashire R.F.U.*
*Coach, Northern Division v All Blacks, 1979*

# Preface

Ray French has already written a book called *My Kind of Rugby*. The book you are about to read should be thought of as our kind of rugby—or certainly how our kind of rugby should be played.

Ray has concentrated on the important years of development—from nine to fourteen—the years in which boys should be building up a repertoire of basic skills, enjoying using these skills and feeling great satisfaction in playing in a game with free expression—not being drilled like robots for the sake of an 'efficient' team.

As coach of the England 19-group schoolboy team, it always pleased me at trials to see the words 'Cowley School' bracketed after the name of the player in the programme. I knew that the player had had a good grounding and would take pride in being a craftsman in his position, whether it be prop or centre.

As this book will be particularly useful for schoolmasters, Ray has not forgotten the importance of administration, and his ideas on a school rugby programme for all ages will be greeted with enthusiasm.

The author played international rugby in a skilful and forthright manner, and the message he has to put over in this book reflects this. It could be the salvation of our game.

**MIKE DAVIS**
*England R.F.U. team coach*
*formerly England Under-19 Schools coach*

# Introduction

The rugby-playing fraternity has become so obsessed with the psychology, philosophy and theories behind the sport that many players and coaches have lost track of its purpose. The national body which controls the game has striven hard to build up a vast network from senior to junior coaches, all with the requisite badges on their tracksuits. Coaching manuals abound which advocate strange types of training methods known as aerobic and anaerobic systems. I wonder if Jeff Butterfield, Bev Risman or Peter Jackson, those magnificently talented players of twenty years ago, ever heard of such courses, badges or systems? I doubt it.

Coaches, I often think for their own prestige, have tried to develop a complicated science out of what is essentially a simple game where all the players should run with the ball. Instead, teams weave intricate patterns of second- and third-phase rugby, always going sideways across the field, drawing men in and out of positions as in chess, but rarely is the scoring of a try the primary function. We should be encouraging youngsters to run and pass the ball with greater freedom, which will allow far more individuality in the game. Hence it is in the youngest players, those from the age of nine years and upwards, that we should instil the correct attitudes to the game.

I make no apology for not producing a highly detailed coaching manual on all aspects of Rugby Union football. The coach or schoolmaster will find little of interest about the collective techniques of forward play such as the scrummage, line-out, ruck and maul, and will look in vain for any discussion of tactics, moves or, above all, the art of kicking a ball. I must stress that my intention in writing the book is to deal with two aspects of rugby football which can be covered by the term 'running rugby', in schools and mini-rugby clubs. I have tried to indicate ways of introducing young boys to the game of rugby in such a way that they get enjoyment from their initiation and appreciate the game as a simple and positive one. I fully acknowledge the values of those features of the game which have been deliberately omitted and agree that later in the young boy's career much work will have to be done on them. My aim is to deal with the arts of running and passing the ball, a return to the original purpose of the game and away from the obsession with kicking.

I fully accept that at senior level kicking can be brought to a fine art, and that players of the calibre of Andy Irvine (Scotland) and Ollie Campbell (Ireland) can dominate a game by their kicking ability. Obviously the stand-off or full-back with the talent to clear his line with a long relieving defensive kick will bring a smile to any coach's face, as will the high attacking punt launched by the stand-off for his threequarter line to follow at great speed. Such use of kicking is for the good of the game, but in order to rid the youngster of kicking indiscriminately I would advise that in the earliest years all kicking be curbed. From the outset a boy will then be aware that running the ball is the player's first priority. Once running and handling skills have been developed it will be easy for the coach to graft on the skill of kicking.

The emphasis in coaching needs to be shifted from collective techniques to individual skills, so that a boy develops a simple and free-running approach to the game by the time he reaches senior level. Above all, coaches should provide fun and enjoyment for the young player from his earliest initiation in the game, and strive to develop a strong competitive instinct so that he is concerned not only with the winning but with the manner of achieving the win—by the scoring of tries.

The coach should enjoy himself too, and much pleasure can be gained from watching a team you have trained perform well during a match. Running rugby is also about organization. I have tried to indicate many areas which the coach should look at, and the many problems which he must be aware of in handling boys and other staff, if he is to manage successfully. Indeed, off-the-field matters are just as important for a coach, schoolmaster or club helper as what happens on the field, for without the correct attitude from those in charge little respect or success will result from the players.

# Key to the Diagrams

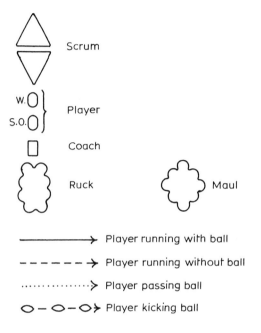

Scrum

w. Player
S.O.

Coach

Ruck    Maul

————————→ Player running with ball

— — — — — — → Player running without ball

················> Player passing ball

○ — ○ — ○> Player kicking ball

# 1. The First Steps

The first games' period in school or the inaugural meeting of the mini-rugby section at the local Union club can be a most unnerving experience for the schoolmaster or organizer who has been delegated to teach rugby to the young beginners. Faced with a vast array of boys in multi-coloured shirts and with boots often two sizes too big for them ('My mum says I'll grow into them!'), the coach often hurls an oval ball to the mass thronging round him and despairingly ponders his first move.

With soccer, when a round ball is thrown to a group of boys the simplicity of the game allows them to grasp quickly the essentials. They cannot handle the ball, but they can kick it forwards, backwards or sideways. A goal is scored when the ball is kicked or headed between posts at either end of the pitch and the team with most goals at the end of the game is the winner. In contrast, Rugby Union football is a more complex game and therefore far more difficult to teach and to learn. A player may kick the ball forwards, backwards or sideways, but sometimes it must bounce and sometimes it need not. He can pass it only behind him. Infringements can result in a kick, a scrum or a tap penalty. But what sort of a kick? Whose scrum? When can a pack leader choose a line-out? Few can pick up the basics of rugby as easily as soccer, for so much must be explained before thirty boys with an oval ball can demonstrate rugby rather than chaos. The coach, however, must realize that the number of players, the complex laws of the game and the skills of the play must all be broken down initially into workable units and then built upon to form a whole. The boys' appetite for the ball must be fed at an early stage. Schools or clubs which sit seventy or eighty eager and enthusiastic boys down behind their desks or on the grass while 'sir', accompanied by a wonderful array of charts, diagrams and magnetic men, deals with the 'dos' and 'don'ts' of the game will fail to satisfy the hunger for rugby.

I find that youngsters are unable to concentrate for more than a couple of minutes without activity, and that hour-long sessions designed to explain the game will do little but leave the youngster thoroughly confused and disenchanted. If the atmosphere is right within a school or club then the boy will be wanting to play. The longer you bore him with the intricacies of binding in the front-row the less inclined will he be to listen and hence take up the game.

## A Workable Unit

I have never met a coach who can teach rugby in the earliest stages to groups of thirty boys, hold their full attention and maintain total participation. A boy must be fully involved from the start, and should have as little as possible on his mind other than the two basic essentials which make rugby so different from soccer:

1. running with the ball.
2. tackling his opponent bodily.

The boys should be divided into teams of seven players, although six or eight a side would be suitable depending on the number of players and staff available. Units, each comprising two teams, should then be set up. They can play across a normal pitch between the try-line and the 22-metre-line, using the touchlines as try-lines. Though a shorter length than the width of the pitch can easily be used, do not make the area wider than the 22-metre-line since such a narrow space affords no hiding place for anybody and all players will be forced into the game.

## The First Game

This is based on the principle that the teams of each unit should start handling the ball immediately. As coach allotted to one unit, you should line out the players as in figure 1 and, keeping both sides ten metres apart, you should stand between them with the ball. The only points to explain to the boys at this stage are that a try, counting four points, is scored when the ball is placed over the try-line and that a player is in touch when he breaks the side lines. All that the boy needs now is to be reminded of two basic essentials:

1. when he is in possession of the ball he must run to score.
2. when not in possession he must stop his opponent from scoring.

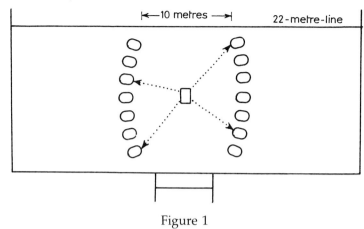

Figure 1

Pass the ball to various players on one side and encourage them to run and to try to score by any means possible—handing-off, crashing an opponent out of the way, swerving, sidestepping or running round him. Insist that the player always goes forward. At the same time urge the other side to stop him by tackling him to the ground.

Do not allow the boy to pass to another in these early stages, but concentrate on the player passing the ball quickly back to yourself when he has been tackled. This will enable you to send off another player with the ball. When six tackles have been absorbed, swap the teams' roles and pass the ball to players on the other side and allow them in turn to attack. Stress the need to run strongly and urge the runner and the tackler by name. Encouragement is important; a little praise does much for a boy's confidence.

After a while, spray the passes from side to side as fast as you can retrieve the ball from the tackled player. Soon they will begin to seek the ball and many will relish the physical contact which is the first hurdle to overcome when learning rugby. Few boys have played the game at primary school and most have only kicked a soccer ball in a game which does not demand the bodily contact needed for rugby. Therefore after ten minutes of running a boy will realize his newly found strength and appreciate his new skills, while others will delight in stopping him. Others may cry and head for the field gates. They will soon be back when you have ignored the cries of 'Ooh, my leg, sir, my leg!' Tears are a natural device at nine, ten or eleven years when faced with difficulties on the field. As a coach you must never pander to the player.

Keep spraying the ball about so that everyone is brought into the game, particularly to the quiet boy on the wing. He may be a natural player or he may not want to know the game. You must find out. Give the ball to a boy with space round him to see if he can run and beat a man and at the same time call a tackler by name to see if he can stop the runner. Set up the personal challenge whenever you can. The boys will respond eagerly. As the boys' confidence and enjoyment grows let the attacking player retain the ball after a tackle rather than pass it back to you. To bring the ball back into play the player can tap it with his foot as in a normal tap penalty (figure 2a) and pass to a team-mate. The tackler should retire a metre and mark the player as in the Rugby League play-the-ball situation (figure 2b). The need to release the ball when tackled can be introduced later—adopted at this stage it will result in a mad scramble and chaos. Allow each side to have six tackles then transfer the ball to the other team. Even though the coach is now out of the game and the players on each side are integrating a little, the boys still need to have only two things on their minds: running and tackling. They will still not know the difference between a ruck and a maul, or a loose-head prop and a tight-head prop, but they will be playing rugby and they will be enjoying the game. The coach need only concentrate on keeping

Figure 2a

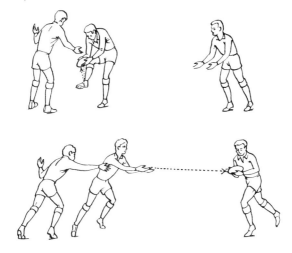

Figure 2b

the two lines ten metres apart. The game can now be expanded, for some boys by virtue of their size and speed will be beginning to dominate the unit.

Many players will enjoy scoring tries, some will relish tackling and the physical contact, while others—notably wing men—will delight in escaping it. Those who avoid tackling may well develop the confidence and ability to make strong challenges as their bodies mature and strengthen. Some, unfortunately, no matter how long the coach strives or how much he varies his approach, will never have the appetite to make a solid tackle. Hopefully their attacking flair will compensate for this deficiency.

## Encouraging Passing

Now is the time to introduce passing, but not at the expense of stopping the game to show the boys the different techniques. As long as the ball passes from player to player let them enjoy it, for any demonstrations will only break up the flow of the game. They will be unable to grasp what techniques you are trying to indicate until they can understand the necessity for them in a real situation.

Still allow a side to retain the ball for six tackles and insist that the player who receives the ball first passes to another of his side before a try can be scored. This simple passing will begin to teach the rudiments of backing up a player with the ball, and will put a stop to the cries of 'Go on Jim, go on' as all Jim's team-mates stand back and urge the side's biggest player to crash through the opposition. After a short time extend the passing and insist on two passes before a player can score. Even if a player has broken through the opposition, make him slow down until support arrives to take the second pass needed before his team can score. Within a short time the boys will be thinking of three skills: running, tackling and now passing.

A further constraint can be put on the players by allowing no one to run more than fifteen metres with the ball before passing to one of his side. This will strike home the necessity of support play and the value of good backing up. As the game progresses the boys will develop a simple understanding of playing and working together as a team.

Infringements—the knock-on, forward pass, or offside and stepping into touch—I would deal with by transferring the ball to the non-offending side and explain the offence while the game is in progress. At this stage it is not vital for young players to know about line-outs, scrums and tap penalties. Players will quickly become conscious of infringements for they will not wish to give the ball away to the other side. The necessity of retaining possession will be uppermost in their minds.

### Release of the Ball in the Tackle

Once the boys have grasped the fundamentals and have begun to enjoy the game, it is necessary to get the player with the ball to release it when he is tackled. This aspect of Rugby Union is one of the most difficult to teach youngsters, for they invariably tend to lie on the ball, hold on to it or bury it under a huge pile of bodies. Everyone seems keen to chase the ball and secure it when loose with the result that there is often no player left to receive it when it has been won.

The law introduced in season 1977/8 which states that 'a tackle occurs when a player carrying the ball in the field of play is held by one or more opponents so that while he is so held the ball touches the ground' has led to far more mauling of the ball than rucking. A player now seeks to retain the ball on his chest or hold it off the ground when tackled, in order to hand the ball to one of

1. Fran Cotton delivers a well-timed pass to a colleague in close support. His ability to pass and handle the ball in open play stamps him as a forward of exceptional class. (England v. France 1977) *Colorsport*

his support players. Since a player has only to release the ball in a
tackle when it actually touches the ground, I would recommend
that you first concentrate on winning the ball with the hands as
opposed to rucking. Apart from the greater control of the ball
when in the hands, it also serves to impress upon the boy that
rugby is essentially a handling game. Leaving aside the unit for a
short while, two simple exercises can be used to practise the
techniques necessary for either retaining or securing possession
of the ball.

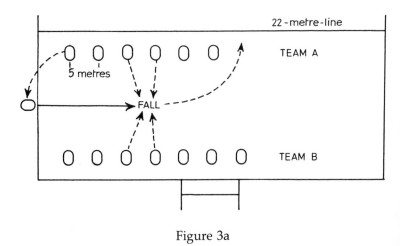

Figure 3a

**Exercise for Basic Mauling**    As illustrated in figure 3a, a line of
six players and a line of seven players should be spaced approxi-
mately five metres apart, facing each other along the try-line and
the 22-metre-line. The seventh player from team A should be
positioned on the touchline midway between the two teams and
instructed to sprint between the two teams, fall to the ground as if
tackled whenever and wherever he wishes and release the ball
facing his team. The player should then roll away from the ball as
he would be expected to do under match conditions. Those
nearest to where he falls should race to retrieve the ball. Urge the
players to grapple vigorously for it, and create a sense of competition by giving points to the side whose players are successful.
The ball can now be returned to the centre of the touchline while
the player who has released the ball following his voluntary
tackle joins the end of his team. The new player nearest the

touchline should be the next to run with the ball. Work through the exercise until all the players of each team have taken their turn at running.

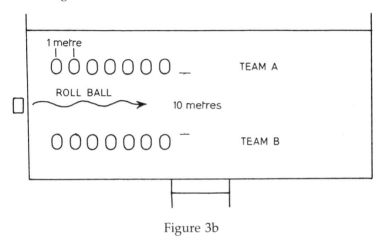

Figure 3b

**Exercise for Mauling and Slipping the Ball**   This is designed to instil the need for more than one or two players to join the maul after a tackle. It will also help in your eventual search for forwards. As in figure 3b, close the spaces between the players to one metre, yet still keep both lines ten metres apart. Roll the ball down the centre of the two teams. Five or six players from each side should converge on the ball and try to pick it up and slip it back. They will soon learn the advantages of driving forward while doing this; however, at this point leave the intricacies of mauling well alone.

   After concentrating on releasing the ball and regaining possession, the techniques can be put into operation in the unit game of seven-a-side. Encourage those nearest to the tackled player to ferret quickly for the ball and to pass it on to others of their side. Many boys who have not emerged as runners may now begin to emerge as ball getters—the future flank-forwards.

## Grading the Units

After four or five sessions, players who are blessed with size, speed or natural skills will quickly emerge. Some players will be extremely aggressive and the weaker boys will soon be out of their depth among them. It is vital that you then divide the units into sets on merit. If this is not done, the stronger and more skilful boys will command the ball and run at and tackle each other, while the weaker players will just become observers on the wings. The strong will receive a false sense of their ability and the weak will lose any appetite for a game in which they find it impossible to compete. Since size is a crucial factor between the ages of eight and fourteen the smaller boy should be allowed to develop at his own pace in a set suitable to his ability. Obviously you should not be too dogmatic when consigning players to a weaker set, for many teams need the small but strong scrum-half and the tricky and squat stand-off. Never dismiss any player when young for many will surprise you later. Dave Carfoot, the Waterloo, Lancashire and England Under-23 scrum-half, was too small for my Under-12 team when at school but that did not deter him from becoming the 1st XV captain and the player he is today. I could hardly pick out Ian Ball (ex-Wasps, Lancashire and England Under-23 and now Barrow R.L.F.C.) above the grass when he was eleven years old; but place a ball in his hands and he could score from anywhere on the pitch.

### Introducing the Elements of the Game

With a balance of players in the sets I would now advocate the introduction of a three-man scrum and a two-man line-out, with the hooker throwing in the ball at the line-out. These forwards will be the ones to encourage to follow the ball and to win it for their side. The boys will now be competitive within their own ability groups and you should be ready to promote or relegate a player as he improves or slackens within his unit. Although rugby is essentially a game played for enjoyment, I feel that as a coach you must never forget that young boys desire competition. Give it to them. At the end of your training sessions you should allow twenty minutes in which teams of seven can play each other on a handicap basis. The matches should last five minutes. The weakest team could be given a twenty-five point lead in each game while the strongest does not receive anything. Such competition gives a tremendous incentive to the strongest team to prove itself the best and for the weakest to achieve something at its expense. By organizing a small league-table for the teams and by giving it full publicity on the school or club notice-boards you will capture the interest of the most important players—that tiny junior is a possible future 1st XV captain.

Having had two training-sessions a week for about a month, the youngsters will be ready to move from the basic rugby of the units to a proper game. Now they possess running, handling and passing skills, they will be in a better frame of mind to receive the laws of the game.

# 2. Developing the Fifteen-a-side Game

Although the young players will by now have mastered the basic skills under competitive conditions, it is not practicable to introduce the fifteen-a-side game immediately. It may require another couple of weeks for the boys to absorb fully the rudiments of match play and it is difficult for a coach to explain the laws if there are thirty players on the pitch. Consequently it is better to have a half-way stage by increasing the units to two teams of eleven players a side. Such teams can produce a simple but effective game that will test most aspects of play eventually required of a boy. The emphasis should still be on attacking and running rugby.

### The Eleven-a-side Game

**The Forwards**  The pack should consist of six players—three in the front row, two in the second row and a No. 8. I would forgo the flank-forwards. Flankers, though excitingly constructive in the senior game, in my experience serve only as a destructive force in these early days. The two youngsters concerned either spoil the play round the half-backs in their eagerness to stop the ball, or hang on the edges of play uncertain whether they are forwards or backs. The first priority is to create the conditions to encourage running half-backs and I feel that less pressure should be placed on them in this formative period. Give them the space and freedom to run and let them develop it as their first instinct in rugby. There is also the need to create a forward mentality of hard graft. Two boys fringing on the sides of a pack to pick up loose balls are surely not wanted until they have learned a forward's basic job.

The six forwards must be encouraged to become a tight pack and to realize that their task is to supply the backs with good ball. Hence, in the game, only the pack should be allowed to retrieve the ball after a tackle. This compels all six to move round the pitch in pursuit of the ball. It stops them from cluttering up the back play and makes the backs think of lining up for the next attack immediately after the tackle. A mad scramble with twenty-two pairs of hands fighting for the ball is therefore stopped. The pack, by hunting for the ball, will always be on hand to support any break by the backs. At the scrums a regular switching round of the No. 8 and second-rows will place greater emphasis on the tackling capabilities of all three and help to develop them, for in the senior game a second-row will rarely make an individual tackle in eighty minutes of rugby. All three will have greater opportunities to handle the ball from the increased scope which is available to a No. 8 breaking quickly away from a scrum.

**The Backs**  These consist of two half-backs, two centres and a wing. The loss of the two flank-forwards not only affords the half-backs greater freedom to run and pass, but places a more urgent need on the stand-off to develop sharper defensive qualities. Too many of our international stand-offs have sheltered behind an open-side flank-forward and merely shadowed an opponent across the field instead of going forward to relish the tackle. A non-tackling stand-off, no matter what his attacking qualities, can be a huge liability. Not enough emphasis in modern rugby is placed on a solid tackler at stand-off who can upset the rhythm of the opposition.

Only one wing is necessary, for even in the best-organized sessions young midfield players cannot keep two wings fully supplied with enough ball. One wing will have plenty of running to do from either side of the field and, in defence, the values of covering are strenuously underlined. The sight of a small full-back with his shirt down to his ankles, his stockings flopping over his boots, standing alone forty metres behind play is a common one on school playing-fields. Leave him out, for it is difficult to involve him fully as yet. Many schoolmasters tend to push the weakest player to full-back; this is not a sensible arrangement for the full-back must be one of the best backs on the pitch to take advantage of today's touch-kicking laws. With eleven players, all are involved in running rugby, and all, especially the three-quarter line, realize the need to tackle, for there is no secondary line of defence in a full-back.

The teams will now be able to play a recognizable form of Rugby Union with the freedom needed to concentrate on running with or passing the ball to score tries. At the same time, each individual, free from thoughts of organized defence, will realize the need to be certain of his own tackling ability.

## Graduating to Fifteen-a-side

With this steady and methodical build-up in numbers of players, each player can approach a fifteen-a-side game knowing at least something of what is required of him and aware of what is needed from others in the field. Each boy will have acquired some sense of the disciplines needed for his position on the field, and this will enable the coach to start a match for thirty boys without the accompanying chaos. The teams should now be eager to run, pass and tackle, and be filled with the competitiveness to provide for a fluent game. The coach, as referee, can 'talk' the players through his decisions and explain any infringement as it occurs. When it is necessary to blow the whistle, ask the offending player why you have blown, or ask a back near to the offence why you have stopped play at the line-out or a maul. Make all aware of the laws as the game flows, being particularly harsh on the offside laws, even to the extent of stopping the game, pointing out the offence and bodily walking the offending player back to an on-side position. If this law is not illustrated at the earliest opportunity every game will be reduced to a shambles.

Once the fifteen-a-side stage has been reached, a coach should not be afraid to select a side to play against external opposition. Although the boys will only have three or four months' experience of rugby under pressure, they will relish the opportunity to represent their school or club and will learn more quickly about their strengths and weaknesses. The coach should not be too selective in his opponents: the unbeaten junior team must not be his sole aim. Players often learn more from a defeat than from a string of easy victories and too much easy success can create faults which are difficult to eradicate at senior level. The success of a coach is not in his unbeaten Under-12, -13, or -14 teams but in his ability to instil in the boys a positive attitude towards the game and to cultivate the skills which will make them good club rugby players.

## Assessing Potential

The coach should always be assessing the capabilities, physique and inclinations of his protégés. The various skills and attitudes

2. As a scrum-half Gareth Edwards possessed remarkable strength and power. Here he displays his strength as he dives for the line through the English cover defence. (Wales v. England 1971) *Colorsport*

they reveal give a good indication of the positions to which they will be best suited. Some players are obviously born to certain positions and this can be apparent even at the age of eleven or twelve. John Horton (Bath, England and Barbarians) when at school was always destined to be a stand-off with his short but compact build, neat sidestep and delicate balance. By virtue of their skill and physique, other schoolboy internationals, such as Mike Burke (ex-Waterloo and Lancashire R.U., now Widnes R.L.F.C.) and David Gullick (Orrell, Lancashire and England trialist), could play at full-back, centre or stand-off. I would be surprised if Mike Burke, now playing Rugby League, does not end his career at loose-forward. Players such as Ian Ball (ex-Waterloo, Wasps and Lancashire R.U., now Barrow R.L.F.C.) and David Carfoot (Waterloo and Lancashire), who toured Canada as stand-off and scrum-half respectively with the England Under-23 party in May 1977, had only played once in those positions while at Cowley School.

Consequently, though various qualities are needed for certain positions, no coach should be too dogmatic in selecting boys for particular positions. Physique is often a controlling factor in the ten to fourteen years age-range. Some boys grow quickly, some do not; some improve in pace, others slow down—with the result that as boys are ever changing, so might their positions. A coach will often only find a boy's true position when, with his team injury-stricken, he is forced to experiment. Certain accepted physiques and attributes are necessary and these are described in most coaching manuals dealing with playing-position requirements. However, some additional observations might be helpful when dealing with this age-group.

**Full-back**  The old established virtues of solid tackling and the ability to kick a ball are only the first, requirements of a good full-back. Nowadays he must also be one of the best footballers on the pitch, possessing the same skills as the stand-off. He is vital in launching attacks or counter-attacks, especially from broken play, and this demands quick thinking allied to nimble footwork.

**Wing-threequarter**  The restrictions on kicking directly to touch outside the 22-metre-line demand a wing who has the ability to link up and make play with his inside backs. He can no longer be a boy who is a mere sprinter and 'finisher off' of movements. The all-round ability of Mike Slemen, the England wing, who is able to pick up a ball in midfield knowing what to do with it, where to run and pass, is to be preferred to the sprinter with only one thought in his head—kick it! An appetite for work in covering across field in defence is priceless and young wings would do well to study Mike Slemen in action here.

**Centre**   'A good big 'un will always beat a good little 'un' is not always true, but at junior schoolboy level this maxim is a good guide and the coach must have one centre who has a physical presence.

**Scrum-half**   Despite all the skills which made Gareth Edwards one of the world's finest players at scrum-half, I believe one of the most important factors in his success was his power. His upper-body strength was so necessary when dealing with the challenges of a back-row, whether in making a break against them or in holding off their tackle while making a pass. The scrum-half must be 'cocky', aggressive and resilient to forwards. The skilled but delicate player has no future here.

**Stand-off**   If you need to search for a stand-off, then you have none! Such players are born, not made. The squat, sidestepping player in the mould of Irishman Tony Ward and Gareth Davies of Wales, or the similarly built England stand-offs Bev Risman of the 1959 British Lions and John Horton today, is the model for the coach. The stand-off must be a natural player who can attack another stand-off, commit his opposing back-row and perform the unorthodox. If you find one, nurture him and avoid telling him the school-leaving age!

**The Front-five**   Front-row and second-row forwards need to work as a unit in a way which is not required of other positions on the field; nevertheless their ball-handling skills must be encouraged. That fatal knock-on from a lumbering prop when confronted with an open line, or the badly timed pass from a second-row in the last minutes of a game, can be crucial. Too many coaches excuse the player with the sympathetic cry: 'He's only a forward.'

**No. 8**   The No. 8 must be the best handler in the pack as he acts as the constructive link between backs and forwards. His ball-handling skills at close quarters are crucial to a game. A big boy who may be a little too slow for the centre is the player to cultivate—one who can open up play with his half-backs.

**Flankers**   Most coaching manuals recommend that flankers play left and right of the scrum, both performing the same functions. Ideally I would agree, but rarely are there two boys in a school team with the same attitude and skills for the job. Consequently I prefer to play open-side and blind-side flankers. The open-side flanker should have speed and ball-handling ability and the vision to create moves in open play. My blind-side flanker has usually been a slower, more solid and ruggedly uncompromising type of boy. I think this is one area of positional play where one can specialize, for it concentrates both flankers' minds exclusively on their role.


## Leadership

With all his youngsters at the learning stage of the game, the coach will dominate the thinking of his players until they reach the age of fourteen or fifteen. Therefore I feel that the captaincy of a team should be given, temporarily, to the most naturally-gifted player. Young boys respect the skills of their friends and look up to such players. A coach will need someone who, in these early days, can lead from the front, for eleven and twelve is not the age for the less able boy to inspire a side from the back. Young boys will gather round the best player and expect to be set an example. As the qualities of other players emerge in the following months do not be afraid to change the captaincy. It can be good for both the team and the individuals and enables the coach to see how they respond and succeed with different types of leadership.

Change is also necessary for coaches. Every fifteen is different and it is good for them to have to adjust to different boys and to sides with different qualities. To have the same junior coach for three or four years can have an inhibiting effect on the players and on the coach himself. A new man is needed each season, one with different emphases and who can look at a player in a different light to the previous coach. He can bring in new recruits to the team and look at the weaknesses of an older-established player. It is vital experience for a coach to have to handle different types of boy and necessary for a boy to have to react to different men.

The coach must remember that in these early years his young players' bodies are still developing, their temperaments are being formed and their commitment to the game of rugby is being tested. A strict disciplined framework for rugby is vital from the coach off the field, but his ideas on his players' abilities and his requirements from them on the field should always be flexible to allow his charges to develop naturally.

# 3. The Importance of Passing

When Peter Squires was selected for England's wing in the Calcutta Cup match against Scotland in 1979 he broke the record, long held by Cyril Lowe, for the most-capped England wing. Yet in twenty-six appearances for his country he had scored only six tries to Lowe's eighteen, scored before and after the First World War. In the early 1920s Carston Catcheside of Percy Park, that genial chairman of the England selectors in my own playing days, scored in every Home Championship match in the 1923/4 season, six tries in all. H. P. Jacob, the other wing, scored a hat-trick of tries against France in the same season, giving a tally of nine tries in one championship season from the wings. During the 1950s and early 1960s that pair of contrasting wings Peter Jackson and the barnstorming Peter Thompson scored eleven tries in fifteen appearances together. Yet by the mid-1960s and 1970s Keith Fielding, Keith Savage and Rodney Webb could only amass four tries from thirty-five appearances. Are we to assume that their predecessors were more skilful and faster? They certainly were not, but such a dearth of tries demands an explanation and I think that it is to be found in the approach to rugby of both player and coach in recent years.

The rapid deterioration in the number of tries scored in international rugby is surely the responsibility of the coaches and selectors in what they demand from a player at the highest level. English rugby in particular has suffered from the malaise of over-elaboration in midfield and from the obsession with playing strong 'crash ball' runners in the centre. One of the saddest sights in rugby for me has been midfield players with few skills indulging in the endless round of 'miss moves', 'switches back to the pack' and 'crash balls', where one centre drives like a battering ram at his opponent or runs sideways back into the opposing flank forwards.

I fully realize that a team must offer variety in attack and seek to break up stereotyped play by the use of moves at the base of the scrum and from the back of the line-outs with the back-row and the half-backs. However, the purpose of pushing in a scrum or jumping at a line-out is to win the ball and take it away from the opposite pack. If eight men have fought for a ball then why take that ball back to the opposing eight forwards and risk losing it at a maul or a ruck? A side should transfer the ball to where there is less concentration of players on the field. Hence the ball should be transferred efficiently to the wings.

That it was not done in the 1970s is due to the emphasis many coaches placed on kicking rather than running rugby. I pity the poor wing. Mike Slemen (England), for example, in the 1979 Ireland v England match touched the ball twice—once when he ran on to the pitch and once when he fielded a kick from the Irish full-back. Is he not entitled to a game as well? British rugby has still not heeded the lesson which was handed out by the touring Australian Schools' team of 1978 which swept unbeaten through the four home countries and, in doing so, delighted countless admirers by the speed and skill of the passing to their strong and speedy wings. I well remember the North of England Schools v Australian Schools match played at Vale of Lune when, though often beaten up front for the ball in the tight play, their inside backs continually transferred the ball to the wings at great speed, giving the wings thirty metres of space in which to work along the touchline. The touring party's whole attitude to rugby was based on passing and running, and, given the dominance of Rugby League in Australia, it was obvious to me where their ideas of back play originated.

As any Rugby League side would, and as I would certainly recommend, the Australian backs lay very flat in attack, bursting powerfully on to the ball and so crossing the gain-line quickly. They also lay very close together with the wing, on many occasions, never more than thirty metres from the scrum-half. Thus, by employing a chain of League-type flick passes, as I would advocate for boys, the ball was in the hands of their fast wings before anyone could move in defence. Given the freedom of the field in which to run, they scored many tries.

In contrast, the emphasis in English rugby has been for the backs to stand deep and wide and for the scrum-half to throw the longest pass he can possibly make in order to take his stand-off partner away from the clutches of the flankers. The length of some of these passes from the base of the scrum has only served to restrict the amount of field available to play in, with the result that on most occasions when the wing receives the ball he has rarely crossed the gain-line and has only two metres in which to work before being pushed into touch. If the backs lie close together then so must the opposition for fear of leaving gaps; if the backs lie flat then they are unlikely to be forced sideways across the field by opposing defences. Speed and accuracy of passing in a short space to give the wing a clear field for running would force a back-row to cover back to the corner flag as they were once encouraged to do. Nowadays the flankers are encouraged to move quickly up into the opposing team's back line, going forward all the time, rather than cover back across the field as they used to do.

Any coach when dealing with youngsters must encourage a handling game. Always stress the need to pass a ball properly and get the players to practise the skills necessary in training-sessions. A coach must concentrate on all his players, forwards and backs alike, and he must not be too obsessed with technique, which I believe has been the major failing of many coaching manuals. The Rugby Football Union's own coaching manual defines a basic pass as 'the method of moving the ball with two hands from A to B in as quick and as effective a manner as possible'. If by the word 'effective' the definition means an accurate pass which places the receiver of the ball in a better position than the passer, then it is obvious that a coach must concentrate on the two essential ingredients of any pass: speed and precision.

Unfortunately with passing, as with most individual skills, many coaches have tended to isolate the skill, teaching the players how to pass without relevance to the actual game. As a result, technique has been rammed down young throats.

'Make sure your right leg is forward. Turn your body at forty-five degrees. Swivel the hip.' These are the cries to be heard on many a field. Forget all this. When you are moving the ball with two hands from A to B what does it matter what position the player's body is in at the moment of passing? Illustrations in coaching manuals have invariably highlighted the positions of the arms and feet, and stressed the thrust from the body needed to swing the arms. All of these so-called vital ingredients will occur naturally if the player is taught to look only at the player to whom he is passing. Our aim is to encourage skills and the Rugby Football Union's manual rightly asserts that 'a skilful passer, in the true sense, is one who times his passes correctly.' Most skills are performed naturally and, in aiming for effective passing of the ball, the coach need only concentrate on the two parts of the body vital to the delivery of an accurate pass: the wrists and the fingers.

3. In early tackling practice, a coach should teach boys to drive their shoulders into their opponents' waists. Here Terry Cobner (British Lions) shows how as he stops All Black Ian Kirkpatrick full-bloodedly, thrusting forward with his shoulders. (All Blacks v. British Lions 1977) *Colorsport*

**The Basic Pass**

The first priority is to encourage young players to grip the ball comfortably and to stress the need for relaxed arms and supple wrists when giving a pass. Make the players stand with the ball cradled in both hands, with the fingers splayed underneath and the thumbs on either side, as in figure 4. The player should move and rotate the ball with his wrists while the coach indicates the need for relaxed bent arms and very loose and supple wrists. Once this has been attained the player is ready to pass.

Figure 4

Most textbooks advocate that the player swings the ball across his body and follows through with his arms so that the power and thrust for the pass come from the body. On the contrary, I would suggest that all the power should come from the wrists with the thrust behind exerted by the flick of the two small fingers on each hand beneath the ball as it is on the point of release (figure 5). As with the Australian Schools' team and universally with Rugby League players, sufficient force will be generated to propel the

Figure 5

ball at speed, and the pass will be quicker than and as accurate as the more orthodox method. The ball must be held and received away from the body to enable a pass, once taken, to be continued at speed along a threequarter-line. Never allow players to hug the ball to the body for it will slow down any movement and restrict their options. Keep the ball always at the fingertips. Make sure that the passer looks at the receiver and passes the ball not directly but a metre in front of him, to make the receiver burst on to the ball and be forced to take the pass with his arms away from his stomach. Concentrate on the hands and wrists and all the 'technique' of the bodily movements will occur naturally.

Obviously passing a ball is an individual skill and initially requires individual attention. It is necessary for a coach to work with a boy as a pair, passing the ball between themselves, or to place the boys in pairs to concentrate solely on giving and taking a pass correctly. However, once they have mastered the basics, I would devise exercises which place the players under pressure by having to pass as quickly as possible or having other players make to tackle them. It is essential to give the young a sense of competition, or boredom and the resultant lack of concentration will set in.

A match, whether in an organized practice-session or against external opposition, is always the best means of testing skills but the following might also be useful for testing passing skills. First, they put a player under the pressure of time, and then of time and opposing players. These will help to instil in a player the ability to time a pass.

## Circle Passing

Divide the boys into groups of six or seven and form each group into a large circle. The ball should then be passed round the circle at speed. While the ball is passing from player to player one member of the squad sets out to run three circuits round the perimeter. Count aloud the number of passes made in the time in which it takes the runner to complete these, making sure to deduct five passes for every ball dropped. Each group will compete with the others to complete the greatest number of passes in the time taken for the circuits, while the runner is gaining good exercise. The boys will strive for speed of passing and will tend to transfer the ball quickly through their fingers, but never allow them to pass sloppily or neglect what they have been told.

## Line Passing

Place the groups behind each other with each player in the first group spaced out along the try-line, the other groups spaced out behind them. Ask the first group to run the full length of the pitch, passing the ball. The front group will, no doubt, run and pass the ball at a leisurely pace, so ask the second group to complete more passes and cover the distance in a shorter time. Now watch the pace hot up! The players within each succeeding group will compete to run faster and pass more quickly and accurately than the previous ones. A boy's failure to give an accurate pass on to which the receiver can run will incur the wrath of his friends in the group. He will soon learn to concentrate.

## Link Passing

Set the groups out as in the previous exercise, with the front group again spaced along the try-line. The first boy of the front group begins the passing and, having passed the ball, he sprints along the line behind the group in order to receive the ball again from the last member of the group's line. The ball should now be passed back along the line and the exercise begun again with the next player. With six or seven players in a line it will be possible to complete the full sequence of passes within the length of a pitch.

## Relay Passing

Space eight players in a line between the try-line and the half-way-line and set two groups of four players, one group on the try-line and one group on the half-way-line, as in figure 6. The two groups of four should hold a relay race while the group of eight should pass the ball up and down its line eight times. The object of the game is to pass the ball more quickly than the runners can cover the distance and it will, if the ball is passed accurately, illustrate the important fact that the speed of a pass will invariably beat the speed of a man. Allow the relay runners to take their turn at passing while those originally passing the ball become the runners. This again will create competition between the two groups.

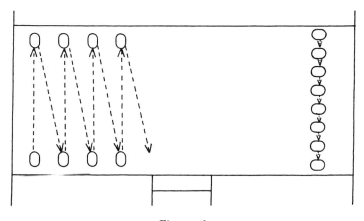

Figure 6

In such exercises, where the players are always conscious of time, the coach should never allow sloppy handling or passing, and should openly praise a well-given or well-taken pass. Following these exercises the coach should try to put his players under greater pressure by introducing opposing players, as in the next exercise, and lastly by trying to simulate all the conditions to be faced on a field when passing a ball in attack.

### Five against Three

Using one half of the pitch, place three players on the try-line beneath the posts with five players scattered anywhere between the 22-metre-line and the half-way-line. One of the group of three should kick the ball upfield to any one of the five players beyond the 22-metre-line. He, on gathering the ball, should link quickly with any of his four partners in an attempt to beat the three defenders to the line by good passing of the ball. Do not allow sidestepping or handing-off. The coach must encourage the speed of the passing to put a player into clear space and must stress the importance of the timing of a pass which will draw the defenders out of position.

### Three-line Passing

As in figure 7, set three groups of five players between the

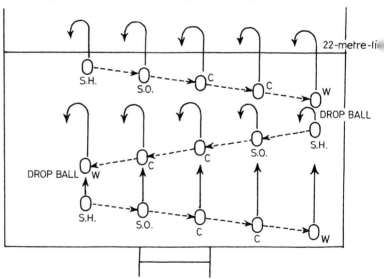

Figure 7

4. Andy Irvine is a full-back who defies the expected. Here he tries to beat two defenders near his own line. (British Lions v. Wellington, N.Z. 1977) *Colorsport*

22-metre-line and the try-line, the boys in each group taking the positions of scrum-half and stand-off, with a wing and two centres. The scrum-half of the front group is given the ball. The front line should start passing the ball while running upfield, with the two groups following behind keeping their alignment at a distance of about fifteen metres. When the wing of the front line receives the ball he must drop the ball behind him and, along with the rest of his colleagues in the line, race forward twenty metres, turn and face the second line as shadowing defenders. The second scrum-half will pick up the ball and begin passing along the second line until his wing, on receiving the ball, drops it behind him for the third scrum-half. The third line should now pass the ball quickly, but it will have to thread its way through players of the other groups as in broken play. Thus all three situations involving line passing in a game are covered—open-field passing, passing against a defence, and passing in broken play.

No exercise can be a substitute for the real game and it is only under full match conditions that a boy's skills in the passing of a ball can be judged. Hence a good pass which splits a defence or is given under pressure in a match should be singled out for the same praise as a good tackle, a shrewd kick, or a well-taken try.

### The Emergence of Forwards

In the early days when the coach has been working with his groups of seven boys he will have formed some ideas as to the eventual field positions of his players. Many, by virtue of their size, are immediately earmarked for the front-five positions of the pack, while others, by their relish for hard tackling and grafting for the ball, quickly find their way into the back-row. Youngsters with forward aspirations, however, must never be treated differently in efforts to cultivate and improve basic skills of passing and running.

To play attacking rugby a team must first win the ball, and thus it is folly if forwards lose sight of their primary role of ball 'getters'; that they are also ball 'users' must be a secondary role. Having been a forward myself I would be the last person to suggest any watering-down of the traditional skills of Union forward play and, especially at schoolboy level, the values of tight forward control cannot be stressed too highly. Many hours must be spent by the boys in learning how to maul or ruck, how to win clean ball from a line-out and how to scrummage effectively. The coach must never skimp on the time spent on the scrum machine, for all young forwards must realize that the collective techniques so necessary to become a sound ball-winning pack are only mastered after constant hard work and rigid discipline. The English Schools' packs of the mid-1970s under their dedicated coach, Mike Davis, certainly illustrated such qualities, as did their counterparts in the senior international side. Unfortunately, though Bill Beaumont, Roger Uttley and the rest of the pack possessed all the ball-winning skills in their Home Championship matches, I fear that, unlike the French, English forwards have rarely equalled players such as Rives, Skrela and Spanghero in their ability to handle a ball and in knowing how and when to make a pass. French forwards, including Celaya, Moncla and Crauste from my own playing days, have invariably possessed that extra layer of skill which makes the complete forward. No back would dare to label them 'donkeys'. All forwards must be able to pass and handle a ball. At crucial times in a match a badly given pass or a dropped ball from a forward can destroy a vital handling movement. Equally the sight of a forward who has caught a ball in midfield, floundering like a beached whale, not knowing what to do, can prove most embarrassing to a player and coach.

## Passing Practice for Forwards

In all his handling exercises and movements the good coach must provide equal opportunities for his forwards to participate in handling movements. In all the exercises I have suggested, only in the later stages should the coach maintain the distinction between forward and back. He should strive to place the forwards in all of the positions and situations normally encountered by a back. However, forwards more often have to handle and pass at close quarters, such as in peeling from a line-out, breaking with the ball from the back-row of a scrum or driving downfield after a kick-off or tap penalty. Thus the coach needs to train his youngsters to pass quickly among each other in a confined space over a distance of twenty to twenty-five metres before, as often happens, they are able to hand on to the accompanying half-backs who should always be snapping at their heels. There is too a need for the No. 8 and scrum-half to practise breaks from the base of the scrum and then involve themselves in close inter-passing with the flank-forwards. The pack can also work peels from the back of the line-out. Such ploys should be attempted until it becomes second nature for each forward to pass to either his left- or right-hand side.

I would always advocate that the running forwards should keep close to the scrum or line-out once they have pierced the initial tackling. They must keep with their support and, in the event of a tackle and ensuing maul, the backs must still have plenty of pitch left in which to run. In a training session a line of corner flags six or seven metres to the side of the scrum or line-out will serve to stop the forwards wandering across the field and keep them on a direct path for the line (figure 8).

Figure 8

Young forwards tire of too much donkey work and yearn for the glamour: encourage them in their running and handling with a couple of exercises designed to help them put three or four passes together in a confined space.

## Fours

Place four forwards at twenty-five-metre intervals along the 15-metre-line which runs parallel to the touchline (see figures 9a and 9b). Each player should have a ball at his feet ready to feed the oncoming scrum-half, accompanied by the other four forwards.

Figure 9a

Figure 9b

Instruct the scrum-half to pick up the ball from each forward's feet. The forward should play it back to him as a No. 8 would. With the first ball the scrum-half passes to one of the four forwards and they must then pass the ball among themselves. All the forwards should have handled it by the time they have covered the twenty-five metres to the next forward waiting with another ball. The process of quick interpassing is repeated to the end of the line with the handling forwards not being allowed to cross the touchline. Keeping them in a confined space will encourage direct running.

## Pick Up and Pass

Split the forwards into two groups of four each with a ball. With one member of the group carrying the ball the players should set off upfield. After ten or fifteen metres the ball carrier should fall, as if tackled, and release the ball on the ground. The nearest forward in the group should immediately pick it up and pass it to the next forward who should in turn pass to the last oncoming forward. This process must be repeated continuously five or six times in the length of a pitch. As well as testing their close passing this exercise will also test the players' fitness since the tackled player will have to get up immediately in order to receive the ball in the next sequence of passes.

Whether it be a schoolboy pack or an international pack, the front-five forwards must be physically strong enough and have been coached in ball-winning techniques to provide sufficient possession for any free running by the backs. If ball-handling capabilities can be grafted on to these accepted forward require-ments then the standard of player will necessarily improve. That forwards of the calibre of Fran Cotton (England), Graham Price (Wales) and Derek Quinnell (Wales) are big enough, strong enough and skilful enough to win the ball, we take for granted. It is their ability to pass and handle a ball when called upon to do so in open play which adds the extra quality that stamps them as players of the highest level. Quinnell's ability to make play from the base of the scrum, Price's ability to give and take a final try-scoring pass, and Cotton's role as pivot in a tap-penalty move all illustrate the value of striving to add that extra layer of skill to forward play. It is hard work but worth it.

# 4. Individual Skills

One of the basic elements in rugby of which a boy must be aware is the value of his own body. Whatever individual skills or team techniques may be developed, the coach must always encourage the junior to realize the full potential of his body in regard to its strength, size and speed. Most youngsters of eight or nine, before coming to rugby football, have only kicked a soccer ball in the park or played at 'three shots at goal' in the street. Few have experienced the physical contact needed for rugby in their kick-abouts and even fewer have used their strength to force their way bodily past another. Such boys will need to gain confidence in their legs and their speed, so that they will be able to beat an opponent by themselves rather than passing on all occasions. Thus, once something akin to a rugby game has been achieved, it is necessary to develop the running and tackling of both backs and forwards, and to assert the need for bodily fitness which even the most skilful players must possess.

Coaches must cast aside the obsessions with crash balls and second-phase rugby which, as I have indicated, have plagued our game for years. After the skilful passing of a ball, the scoring of tries in rugby is about one boy beating another boy by whatever running skills he has—by the use of the sidestep, swerve or, now too rarely, the hand-off. Many coaching manuals, including the Rugby Football Union's own *Guide for Coaches*, in their desire to create free-running backs, stress the need to practise these skills and suggest various exercises to develop them.

## The Sidestep

would disagree with most authorities who say that it is possible to teach a player the movement. They suggest that the sidestep, which takes the attacking player inside or outside the defender, is carried out merely by driving the outside leg into the ground vigorously in order to change direction round the opposing player and then by accelerating away from him. Such a technique is no more than a simple change of direction and all the exercises designed to make boys sidestep corner flags or tackling bags will merely achieve this.

I firmly believe that no coaching will develop the proper side-step, for it is an instinctive reaction in a boy which is there at nine or ten years of age and remains for life. The sidestepping arts of Tony Ward (Ireland), Gareth Davies (Wales) or Peter Squires (England) were produced at birth, just as were the abilities of two of my own ex-pupils, John Horton (England) and Ian Ball (England Under-23, now Barrow R.L.F.C.). They could sidestep at eleven years of age when they were not much over four feet tall. If you do not have a player who can sidestep then you will not suddenly produce one.

## The Swerve

As effective a skill is the swerve; indeed it is possibly even more effective than the sidestep since it takes the runner, usually a back, away from the defender on the outside and away from the cover to the wings. The slowing down in pace by the attacker, followed by the feint towards the defender and the ensuing rapid acceleration away from him, will often create the most desired of all breaks in the opposition ranks—the outside break. Young wings and centres, particularly an outside centre, should be encouraged to develop a swerve by regular practice.

Place a couple of flag posts at intervals of about forty metres along a touchline to act as defenders for the young players to

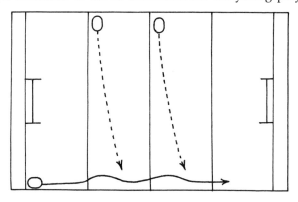

Figure 10

5. Today a wing three-quarter must have all-round ability. He must not only be able to pick up the ball in mid-field, but also know when to run and pass, and be able to cover across field in defence —skills which England wing Mike Slemen displays to perfection and which young wings would do well to study. Here Slemen rounds an opponent to launch a counter-attack. (England Under-23 v. Tonga 1974) *Sport and General*

approach, then feint towards and accelerate away from, in turn. Perhaps a better and more realistic exercise is to station a boy with a ball on the corner of the try-line and touchline and two boys on the opposite touchline, one of them on the 22-metre-line and one on half-way as in figure 10. The sprinter with the ball must set off to score at the other end of the field while the two others act as the defenders by covering across the pitch. The wing must be restricted to swerving round both defenders as they cover deep across the pitch and under no circumstances must he be allowed to cut inside. The tacklers will bring an air of reality and the necessary physical contact which the corner flag posts cannot.

### The Hand-off

The exercise described above can also be used to encourage the use of the hand-off. This is a dying art as many backs and flank-forwards seem to be encouraged in the art of deliberately taking the tackle in order to set up second-phase ball. The attacker should approach the would-be defender with the ball held by the arm furthest away from the tackler and with his free arm bent. On approaching the defender he should straighten his arm with as much force and vigour as possible and, with the open palm, push himself away from the tackler. As in the previous exercise, a restriction should be placed on the runner, namely that he can only use a hand-off in beating the opposition who will be covering across the field.

Rugby is about scoring tries, and the sooner we move away from the reliance on penalty goals and long periods of kicking for position on the field, the better the game will be. Encourage the boys to run and to take on their opponents with a neat sidestep, a swerve or a hand-off. What does it matter if they are tackled as long as they are going forward and attempting something positive in attacking play? Let the youngsters run and handle the ball and they all will enjoy the game: let the youngster kick the ball and only he will enjoy the game.

### Tackling

The other individual skill so necessary to be developed in a player is his ability to tackle. Some boys relish the physical contact, others do not. Some players I have known would not tackle and some could not, but because of other skills they deserved a place in any side. Do not discard a boy who is not a good tackler before you have had a chance to assess his value to the side. Beware though—one is enough for any side to carry.

As a coach, you must stress the need for effective tackling, with the boys instructed to drive forward into their opponent's body and to make impact with their shoulders in the area of the waist. In the steady build-up from the early training-exercises to the actual games, I have restricted the area of play so as to make bodily contact the rule rather than the exception. Cultivate in the players a desire to tackle and to hunt for the player over the field. I firmly believe that just as a player may take delight in running, so a player can derive great pleasure in executing a perfectly timed tackle. In Rugby League, where the attacking players are in possession of the ball for longer periods than their counterparts in Union, I loved a period of play which called for a considerable number of tackles to be made and I received just as much pleasure from it as in running with the ball.

In early training, a coach need only strive to see that the boy brings his opponent down. Do not be too specific in the different types of tackle—behind, side or front—and their execution. Enjoyment should again be the keynote: as a start, the old standby game of 'British Bulldog', as well as being plenty of fun, is a good initiation into the principles of sound tackling. Place two boys midway between the try-line and the 22-metre-line, facing the touchline. At a whistle from the coach the group should attempt to run to the other touchline, at the same time avoiding the two tacklers in the middle. Those boys who are tackled should join the two in the centre for the next charge of the group. As the numbers in the middle increase so it becomes more difficult for the runners to avoid a tackle. Such a game will teach boys how to give and take knocks and how to bring their opponents down.

## One Tackler against Ten Attackers

This is a more strenuous exercise than 'British Bulldog', and can also strengthen a boy's competitive instinct. Place one boy between two flag posts set only ten metres apart and line up ten boys opposite him ten metres away. Such a lack of space prevents anyone running round the boy in the middle and so causes the attacker to run at him. Send the boys through the space in quick succession for the centre boy to tackle them and, as soon as he has made one tackle, though he may still be on the ground, call the next runner. Make the tackler leap up quickly from the ground to make another tackle, giving him no time to relax in between, until he has made or missed ten tackles. Note who tackles the most in the group. Do not bother about the positions of the arms, the head or the shoulder. As long as the boys drive their shoulders into their opponents' waists and thrust forward the coach should be content.

## General Fitness

The freedom to run and the resulting enjoyment for the young player must always be uppermost in the coach's mind. Yet, despite all the skills of handling, passing, running and tackling which he needs to encourage, he must stress the need for the players' physical fitness. Without this the skills will never flourish. Most young players of this age are naturally fit but many are still overfed. No matter what their physical state it is vital that the coach impresses upon his players at an early age that natural skills will only take a boy so far and that as he grows up his personal fitness will be a crucial factor in his success as a rugby player.

For training sessions I always prefer an outdoor circuit which can cater for upwards of forty boys on a full-sized pitch. The circuit should take in at least five exercises which will test all of the boys' footballing skills and at the same time improve their fitness. With two staff in charge, five groups of eight can easily be set out on the pitch as in figure 11. Each exercise is performed for five minutes with one minute allowed for changeovers. Both staff should be moving round the pitch from exercise to exercise, urging the boys to maximum performance.

## Outdoor Circuit

**Exercise 1**   Seven boys are stood in line passing the ball, while the eighth, the runner, tries to race the ball down the line. The passing of the ball should begin with a shout from the player as he starts to run. The exercise should continue until each boy has taken his turn at sprinting.

**Exercise 2**   Six fifty-metre sprints between the flag posts.

eth Davies (Cardiff and Wales) is a natural sidestepper whose skills in
spect are almost certainly instinctive. *Sport and General*

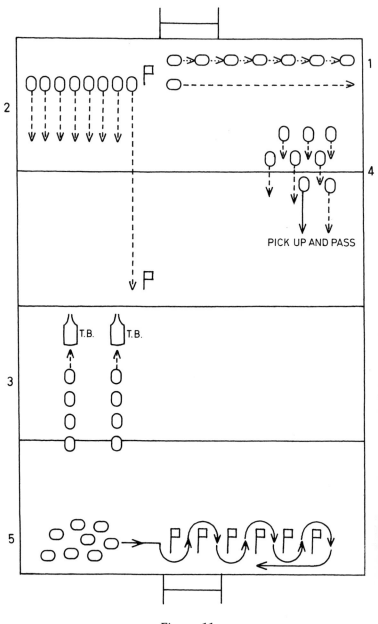

Figure 11

**Exercise 3**   The group should divide into two units of four and proceed to run and tackle tackling-bags in order, the boys concentrating on placing their shoulders hard into the bags.

**Exercise 4**   Pick up and pass. The boys should carry out this exercise as explained in chapter 3, running full lengths of the field during the time allowed.

**Exercise 5**   Each boy in turn, with the ball in his hands, should race and swerve in and out of the flag posts, turn at the last and sprint back to the waiting line. On his return he should pass to the next in line in order to recommence the exercise.

Such a circuit with simple exercises will be far from demanding in terms of physical-fitness training for boys of this age-group but will create a pleasant blend of hard work and enjoyment. The important benefit will be the development of the correct attitude to training before, in later years, the really hard slog of fitness work is required.

# 5. Team Skills

Though we have concentrated on the individual skills and the physical fitness of the youngsters, it is also important that the boys practise running, passing and tackling in an actual game. The players must be placed under pressure from semi and full opposition in a well-organized session which will stretch their physical fitness, test their individual skills, yet bring all the fifteen players of a team together as a workable unit. Such sessions should probably last for about one and a half hours if they are to provide a full test for the boy. The coach must strive to offer him competition and variety as he seeks to involve all the skills that the boy has learnt in the school games' periods or the mini-rugby club's Sunday-morning sessions.

Taking thirty boys and two staff as an ideal unit, the first thirty minutes can serve as a warm-up period in which the boys' passing is put to the test and strong running is a necessity.

**Competitive Touch Rugby**

The thirty players should be divided into two teams of eight and two teams of seven with one side of eight boys playing against one side of seven on a full-size pitch. I would prefer the sides to be unbalanced in order that one team might have the attacking edge and have a sufficient number of players to be able to create overlaps by the simple function of drawing an opponent and then passing to a better-placed companion. The team with only seven players will thus be forced to cover across the field and must learn to cope with a situation in which one player is opposed by two. This is all to the benefit of their defensive thinking. A full-size pitch might seem a vast space for nine- to fourteen-year-olds, particularly after the areas recommended in chapter 2 for their introduction to the game. Such a pitch, though, will give them the space in which to run and create gaps for the attackers. I would never advocate that the sides be split into backs and forwards, a feature of many impromptu games of touch rugby. Such a selection achieves little other than to make forwards feel inferior in loose play and only serves to highlight the differences between the two groups. Balance the teams carefully with a mixture of forwards and backs so that all players run and handle together.

Forwards will have to link in passing movements with backs, imposing on them the need to think in open play far away from scrums and line-outs. Create in the forward a desire to run the ball and thus add an extra dimension to his game. Start both games of seven versus eight and allow a side's players to be 'ticked' (touched) five times before being compelled to give the ball to the other side. By allowing a side to keep the ball for a long time the players are able to maintain handling movements and involve all the team's players. At the same time their opponents' defence can be stretched for a lengthy period. Only blow the whistle for a forward pass or a knock-on and continually keep the two sides ten metres apart at the play-the-ball situation (see figure 2b in chapter 1) following the touching of a player.

After ten minutes, decrease the number of 'ticks' allowed to three and then after a further ten minutes to one. This reduction in the time a side is allowed to possess the ball will make the players concentrate on the speed of their passing and the need to beat a man by good passes. This will help to make a player more creative and help to speed up his reactions as he searches for the gap. Allow the winners of the two games to play each other in order to create a competitive spirit among the players, for such games will aid their fitness work and thoroughly prepare them for the other more physical aspects of their sessions.

## Unopposed Rugby (thirty minutes)

The boys must now learn to come together as a fifteen-man unit. They must realize quickly how the various individual roles of the players complement one another in a team. A session of unopposed rugby—a team playing with the ball but without any opposition—is necessary in order to help them understand their positional play and alignment on a field. However, I would frequently introduce one or two ploys, as outlined later, so that a player never loses his individuality and flair. Many authoritative voices are raised against unopposed rugby, stressing that all the physical contact is taken away resulting in a lack of urgency in the player in possession of the ball. 'Players must pass and run under pressure from the opposition' is one well-worn theory. However,

I believe that boys aged nine to fourteen must first learn to run and pass as a fifteen, free from an opposition to gain their first understanding of the role of the players round them. In these initial stages they will have enough to concentrate on without thinking about the opposition. Having divided the group into two separate fifteens on two pitches, each with a coach, the only things to stress before beginning are the need for simplicity in the backs and support from the forwards.

## Simplicity and Support

The coach should line the side up as in figure 12 with the forwards bunched near the touchline awaiting a 22-metre drop-out. At the drop-kick the pack sprints to the ball and should then use close interpassing to transfer it up the field. The forwards must keep within twenty metres of the touchline so that they run straight and not across the field. Thus in a match they would be penetrating deeper and deeper into their opponents' territory and not merely moving sideways into covering defenders.

Encourage all the forwards to be involved in the passing which should be at their own pace. When they are about ten metres from the try-line, they should form a maul and transfer the ball, via the scrum-half, to the backs who have been following their progress upfield. The simple transfer of the ball at speed to the openside wing is all that is necessary at this stage, but make sure that he puts the ball firmly over the line at the corner, for he must realize his job is to score tries. Repeat this exercise two or three times before starting play with a kick-off from the half-way-line with your kicker aiming to place the ball just on the 10-metre-line for his forwards to rush on to. The distance in which the forwards can pass the ball is now severely restricted, but still insist on all eight players handling the ball before they approach ten metres from the try-line. They will now need to speed up their close passing and back up much more quickly. A good suggestion is to shout the numbers one to eight so that a forward quickly responds to take the ball on a number (not necessarily his own) and soon learns to appreciate the need for timing and close support. The ball can then be transferred to the backs as previously explained.

The final part of the exercise should begin with a short drop-out on the opponents' 22-metre-line. With such a short distance for the forwards to cover before releasing the ball to the backs at the

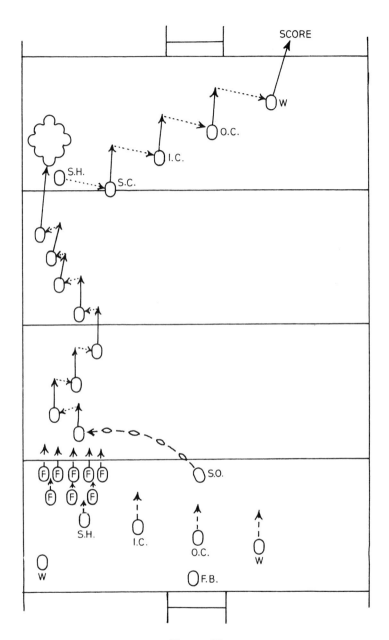

SCORE

W

O.C.

I.C.

S.H.

S.C.

F F F F F

F F F

S.O.

S.H.

I.C.

O.C.

W

W

F.B.

Figure 12

try-line, they are brought under tremendous pressure to slip or pass the ball at speed among all eight of them inside about twenty metres. It can be done, but the coach must shout his numbers to urge his forwards to move and think at speed. The backs, too, must pass the ball along the line more quickly for the coach should insist that only the openside wing places the ball over the try-line. Insistence on this will firmly plant in the young player's head the need to transfer the ball at speed to the wings.

By decreasing the space in which to work the pressure on forwards and backs is quickly increased. This will instil in the players the necessity for close support of each other and the need for slick handling. The coach can now ask for closer support from the forwards by introducing a disruptive factor into the flow of the ball. He should set up a scrum or a line-out against imaginary opposition where the team will win the ball and proceed to pass upfield along their threequarter-line. The full-back should join the line outside the outside-centre and on receiving the ball at the blow of a whistle he should roll it ten or fifteen metres in front of him. The forwards should all be coming across field so call one by name to pick up the ball and begin close passing with another named forward. On reaching a suitable attacking position, they can hand to the backs, who will have re-formed and who must, by quick passing, allow the wing to place the ball over the try-line. Shout a forward's name only as the full-back receives the ball and try to pick a slow-running player who is trailing behind.

The coach must jolt his forwards out of a slow trot across the field and create a sense of urgency in their need to support a player or a breakdown in play. In repeating such an exercise be careful to vary the names called to pick up the ball and to receive the first pass so that all will eventually sprint to the breakdown. As a variation, make the full-back pass the ball inside to a supporting forward (usually a back-row) and make the forward roll the ball for the next one to pick up. In these exercises the coach will have indicated the need for simplicity and support from all the members of the team. In particular, his pack will have been introduced to their role of ball winners, ball getters and finally ball users.

Young players at this age are keen to take part in a series of set moves, and I would feed their appetite for this and improve their confidence. Moves compel a player to discipline himself to set procedures and they also instil the need to work in harmony with other players of the team. I would also recommend moves which

ean-Pierre Rives, France's captain from 1979, is a fine open-running tor-
d in the French tradition of speed and athleticism which brings pleasure to
vds all over the world. *Colorsport*

involve the full-back and wings: at ten and eleven years of age these players can be the forgotten elements of a team, receiving little ball in a match. Quite often a winger at this age tends to be a good runner who does not at first relish physical contact and he needs to be brought fully into the side or he will waste away. I would therefore suggest that you use three standard but simple moves involving both forwards and backs and incorporate them as soon as possible in these unopposed and later opposed sessions.

### 'Me and Thee', 'Thee and Me'

The scrum-half puts the ball into the scrum and at his call of 'me and thee' the No. 8 detaches himself from the scrum and accepts a short pass from the scrum-half. On the call of 'thee and me' from the scrum-half, the No. 8 picks up the ball at the base of the scrum and passes to the scrum-half who will have gone round him to receive the pass. The first word 'me' or 'thee' will signify who picks up the ball (figure 13).

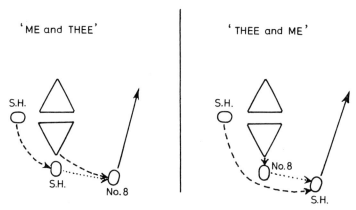

Figure 13

### Dummy Run

From a scrum the scrum-half passes to the stand-off who is lying flat and close. On taking the pass the stand-off turns his back on the opposition and moves sideways slowly towards the scrum while the scrum-half runs round him, closely followed by the No. 8. The stand-off allows the scrum-half to go past him and continue along the line as a decoy and instead slips the ball to the No. 8 who must drive from the gap between the opposing stand-off and inside-centre. The scrum-half should be supporting him on the outside (figure 14).

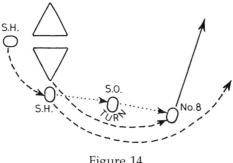

Figure 14

## Wing and Full-back Link

From a scrum, line-out or maul, the stand-off passes to his inside-centre and loops round him without taking the ball from his partner who again turns his back on the opposition to shield the ball. The nearside wing and the full-back must sprint on either side of the inside-centre who is thus able to pass to one player while the other acts as decoy to the opposing flank-forwards (figure 15).

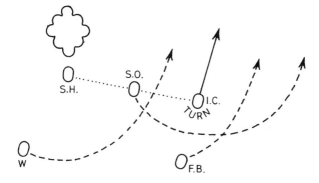

Figure 15

Such moves will give added variety to the training-sessions, and young boys will delight in carrying them out perfectly. However, players must never be slaves to systems, and though there is certainly a need for planned moves and tactics we must not create programmed players for the future. I would hope that the coach moves away from a total reliance on planned moves, particularly the dreary crash-ball tactics which take play back to the forwards, or the deliberate setting up of second-phase rugby. Second-phase rugby should occur by accident when a player is tackled and not deliberately by a player seeking a tackle.

The coach should place a considerable amount of pressure on the individual player to make him use his own personal skills, yet at the same time remember the boy is part of a team. Consequently the coach ought to act as a disruptive element in un-opposed sessions, creating situations where the player will be forced to think for himself and use his skills. For example, place yourself in front of a player who is about to receive the ball and then get him to pass to you. Now punt the ball forty or fifty metres downfield, roll it sideways along the ground or bounce it behind him. Any one of such actions will cause a total breakdown in the flow of the team and cause individuals to think for themselves, retrieve the ball and start again from broken play. Players will have to support others with the ball, some will have to realign themselves, while others will be looking to link up in an impromptu movement. Continue the movement until an infringement occurs or a try is scored. The boys will now have confidence in their handling and running and each should be aware of his capabilities at rugby. Opposition is now essential and the coach should bring both fifteens together for a final thirty-minute session of organized, opposed rugby. Now the boys can use all their new-found moves and concentrate on support play. Above all, each individual will have the opportunity to use his own talents.

## Opposed Rugby (thirty minutes)

Allow one side to have possession from a number of set situations (experience has shown that six is the ideal number) as in figure 16, making both teams sprint to each situation as an infringement occurs. Thus the session is part of the boys' physical training as well. Do not indicate to the team in possession what to do with the ball, but allow them to think for themselves. Let them include

8. The remarkable balance of Tony Ward, Ireland's stand-off, here enables him to round an opponent close to the touchline. (England v. Ireland 1978) *Colorsport*

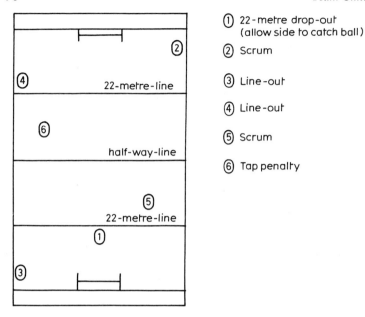

① 22-metre drop-out
   (allow side to catch ball)

② Scrum

③ Line-out

④ Line-out

⑤ Scrum

⑥ Tap penalty

Figure 16

planned moves or use simple passing to beat the opposition and do not discourage individuals from making a break—do not impose any set pattern on them. With one team attacking continuously from the set situations, the defence of the other side will certainly be tested both from the set pieces and from any ensuing play following the breakdown of a movement. When one side has used up its possession reverse the roles and allow the defenders to take their turn with the ball.

Following both sides' attempts with the ball, call a halt and discuss with the players why they carried out a particular move. Criticize or praise an individual's reactions during play and suggest what might be attempted in similar situations, but do not totally impose your thinking on the player. Remember, if an Andy Irvine can defy the accepted on the field and make a break on his own line then allow your players, however young, to do the same. After the short discussion, play a further six set situations, only this time with any side winning the ball and having to attack or defend accordingly. This will quicken the boys' thinking and will place them in a situation as near as possible to the game itself. Each player ought now to have realized that simplicity is often a virtue, that the support of fourteen other players is vital and that, above all, great rugby is about an individual thinking for himself and often doing the unexpected.

# 6. Rugby for All

## All Shapes and Sizes

For any boy involved in rugby there are obvious educational benefits to be gained from travel and in meeting others. Physical fitness, a sense of achievement at having mastered a complex game, and team spirit are accepted virtues. There is also the added advantage that a match involves thirty players —considerably more than other team games. Rugby is one of the few sports that can accommodate all sizes and all temperaments of boys. In soccer, players must possess a certain basic speed and this generally puts them in a well-defined weight-range. If they are too heavy they become ungainly for a sport in which the emphasis is on speed of thought, allied to speed of foot. Conversely, rugby has places for all manner of boys—the tubby, slow prop-forward, the hard, chunky wing-forward and the elegant sprinter on the wings. Here the small scrum-half can play on the same terms as the towering, heavyweight second-row.

## Coaching

In schools, coaches may well be drawn from the physical-education department and thanks to colleges such as Loughborough and Madely, for example, there is no shortage of P.E. teachers well versed in coaching the game. However, in a large school other members of staff must be encouraged to take an active interest in the sport if it is to be organized effectively at all levels. Often the non-P.E. man can devote more time to the team in his charge than can a sports master. And it is refreshing to have a man who is able to come to the game as a form of relaxation from teaching academic subjects and who can assist the P.E. specialist teacher.

Obviously the main priority is to have a member of staff responsible for the coaching of each team, and in this area those in overall charge should not be afraid to take the plunge with someone who knows little about the game but who is enthusiastic. No matter what his weaknesses in the technicalities of rugby, the keen man with drive who will turn out with the youngsters two or three times a week is the best man. The expert or the knowledgeable talker who coaches from the staff-room window may offer his help for years but will only retain the boys' interest for a few weeks. If sufficient support can be raised, allocate two coaches to each team and try to develop two teams—an 'A' and 'B' side—in each year level.

The weaker 'B' XVs can play other school 'B' XVs or weaker opposition first teams. No matter what the teams' standards you are providing a further fifteen to twenty boys with enjoyment and a coach with a sense of involvement and hence achievement.

Apart from the games' period the boys must have a couple of extra training-sessions a week. These extra-curricular sessions are vital whatever the state of the weather. Your teams have to train in all weathers to be able to play in rain, cold and mud. A warm sports hall may be fine for staff on wintry evenings, but you need to know who does not relish the harsh climate and who lacks application when confronted with difficulties from the elements.

In the early stages of teaching youngsters rugby many schoolmasters merely practise and organize matches within their own school—House or Form matches—and often allow a year's grace before subjecting their teams to external opposition. However, what does it matter whether the players do not know all the complications of the laws? Let the boys play for the school against outside opposition as early as possible. If the referee can 'talk' both sides through a game, then engage in matches within a couple of months of the first teaching session. Let the players feel important in their school jerseys; give them every encouragement in their progress and, above all, illustrate the importance and pride in playing for their team.

Play as many matches as possible, for only in a keenly contested game will a boy appreciate his strengths and weaknesses. His appetite for rugby will grow when he observes the rewards of his practices. If staff availability for such practices or matches is at a premium I would advocate the use of senior players from the school's 1st XV alongside the juniors. I have often used such players on a rota basis who have been willing to give up a couple of private-study periods or who are able to help after school. The older boy enjoys the chance to air his knowledge to the juniors; he feels important. The young ones like to be attended by their heroes among the seniors and they will listen intently. With the emphasis on running rugby and a well-organized coaching structure the boys will benefit from the continuity of approach as they rise through the school. The overall standard of play can do nothing but improve.


## Involving Other Help

Apart from the enthusiasm a coach may put into teaching youngsters rugby, in order for the game to flourish he must have support from others off the field. Here it is a good idea to involve teachers who might have only a peripheral interest in the game but who would none the less be willing to help. An art master, for example, can help produce fixture cards and posters and other members of staff can organize the booking of coaches and after-match catering.

Publicity within and outside the school is a crucial ingredient in creating the right atmosphere and in gaining the attention of boys. A large and colourful notice-board displaying team sheets, posters advertising future matches, press reports, coaching leaflets and any other rugby material is needed in a position where everyone will see it. The board must be kept up to date with interesting items culled from magazines and programmes. Publicize the activities of former pupils as an incentive to the present players. If the local newspaper takes match reports then make sure that your teams are represented, for a boy likes to see his name in print and everyone likes the school to be mentioned.

Failing the local press, organize a small monthly newspaper within the school, containing reports on outstanding matches written by the boys themselves, crosswords, quizzes and short articles on personalities. A few hundred copies can easily be cyclostyled, stapled together and sold to aid the rugby funds. Again other members of staff can be involved to help the boys edit the paper. There are also ways of drawing the attention of non-playing pupils. A photographic competition, for example, can easily be arranged with pictures taken on any aspect of rugby. Pin up all the entries on the notice-board. It all adds to the atmosphere off the field.

By using some of these methods you will create a sense of importance about the game in the school. Such measures can be supplemented by ensuring that all match results are announced

9. Close support—among forwards and between forwards and backs—is essential in modern rugby. Here Steve Fenwick, the Welsh centre, looks for support as he is tackled by French forward Jean-Claude Skrela. (Wales v. France 1978) *Sport and General*

in assembly and that outstanding players, on gaining representative honours, are presented on stage. Colours can also be
awarded for outstanding service in the school jersey. With these
incentives you should have no difficulty in recruiting new
players.

## Support from Parents

'But he'll get hurt playing that game. Have you seen all the cuts
and bruises on those players in the international matches on
television?' When fond mothers can often be heard expressing
concern for their nine-, ten- or eleven-year-old offspring it may
seem strange that rugby should have spread so widely in schools.
Yet most parents' views change rapidly in favour of their sons
playing the game. Encouragement from this quarter is a bonus
you must seize, but be careful to keep parents away from selection, team talks and especially the dressing-room. By their nature
they will readily overestimate the abilities of their sons and insist
on their inclusion in the side. Some diplomacy on the coach's part
might be called for. You must remain unbiased or you will lose
the support of the players if the team includes boys simply
because their parents say they are good enough. Allow parents to
channel their energies into areas where they will be most useful—in fund-raising, helping with catering after matches and
assisting with transport to away fixtures.

## School and Rugby Club

The other important source of support which every school should
try to win is the local rugby club. As the game progresses through
the 1980s I believe clubs must take local schools under their wing
and perhaps help them with cash or helpers in return for recruits.
Such a relationship can work to the benefit of both parties. Within
my own area of south-west Lancashire we have received tremendous support from clubs such as St. Helens R.U.F.C. which have
provided their premises for parents' fund-raising functions and
their pitches for special matches, often against foreign opposition, at which we could take good gate receipts. Orrel R.F.C.,
too, have kindly loaned their pitch and floodlights for Cowley
School's use in a prestigious match while Waterloo R.F.C. has
held raffles and sold magazines on our behalf. All the clubs have

built up a welcome relationship with the school and all have benefited from the many ex-Cowleians in their ranks.

## Fund-raising

In order that rugby can develop fully it needs sufficient funds. Boys will provide their own boots and kit for training, but often a school will provide match kit. With shirts costing between £8 and £15, and transport bills ranging from £30 to £50 for a Saturday away game, few coaches can afford to relax on the sports allowance from their headmasters or Local Education Authorities. The financial burdens of rugby can be crippling and therefore it is up to everyone involved in the game to think up ways of raising money to pay for the extra fixtures, after-match refreshments, new kit and the like.

The world of fund-raising is no place for the shy, introverted schoolmaster or club helper for it must be approached with a hard mercenary outlook. To reap the rewards, a person needs to assume the role of salesman, impresario and agent. With this combination of talents the following suggestions are worthy of consideration as ways of raising money.

**Collection of Waste Paper**   Having humped and loaded over two hundred tons of waste paper over the years I would advise this method be adopted only as a desperate resort. Watch the sharp price fluctuations at the collectors which can rise and drop alarmingly according to demand for recycled paper. A large amount of work is involved for the money raised, but since there is no expenditure all returns are profit. If the coach knows a friendly travel agent who will let him have all his summer tour brochures at the end of the season then the coach should be on to easy money. But it's never that easy. On one occasion at my own school I was approached by a small grimy-faced player after a strenuous fund-raising effort.

'Sir, sir . . .'

'Shut up a minute. Put that box of paper on the corner of the lorry.'

'But, sir, I've . . .'

'Hurry up, it'll hold the weight of all that cardboard in the middle,' I observed as I sat back at the side of the lorry surveying the ten tons of waste paper neatly stacked. Ten tons of waste

paper at £15 per ton, another £150 for our funds. I wiped my
brow of the sweat of two hours' work and waved a fond farewell
to the lorry about to disappear through the school gates. The
boys, who had been strung out in chain-gang fashion passing
bundle after bundle of newspapers and old cardboard, now
strained their ears for the four o'clock bell which would signal
their release.

'But, sir . . .'

'What's the matter, Taylor?'

'Sir, I put my coat down on the lorry when we started and now I
can't find it.'

My eyes rolled to heaven at the thought of a school blazer
beneath ten tons of waste paper on its way to be pulped, and I
thought to myself: 'What the hell am I doing here? What's it all
about?'

But never forget that it's all about rugby!

**Sponsored Matches**   Those who have tried to organize a sponsored walk, run or jog in the pouring rain and have had to take
precautions to stop hundreds of schoolchildren from falling
under articulated lorries will surely welcome something easier.
May I suggest a sponsored match. Get the players to badger
parents, brothers and sisters and friends into giving them a
certain amount of money for every point their team scores.

**A Boxing Evening or Concert**   Why not become an impresario
for an evening and don the suit of the master of ceremonies by
hiring a hall or theatre and putting on a show by local pop groups,
artists or even a boxing club.

**Sportsman's Evening**   A dinner organized in the local rugby
club followed by speeches from three guest-speakers from the
rugby world or sport in general is an easy money-spinner and one
which can even be enjoyed by the organizer. By adding a couple
of pounds per head to the cost of the meal and by seeking
sponsorship from local industry or commerce to pay the expenses
of the guest-speakers a hefty profit can be made. Contact a local
radio station's D.J. to act as the compère.

**A Charity Shop**   If you have an ex-pupil who has become a
successful estate agent, ask him to loan you a shop in the town
centre for a week. By placing request letters through people's
letter-boxes in various areas of the town about a fortnight before,

you will be surprised by what you will obtain in your requests for clothes, furniture, household goods, books and the like. The goods received will raise huge profits—over £1,500 in a week is possible—and the venture will provide fun and companionship for staff, boys and parents (serving in the shop during the day) and bargains for the shoppers.

**Hire of a Train**   The hire of a train for a day trip to London, Edinburgh or the seaside, for example, is a novel form of fund-raising. Even allowing for British Rail's costs, you can still charge less than the normal fare and end up with a profit. Selling your own refreshments on the train can also boost funds.

**Magazines and Newspapers**   Brochures, magazines and especially a sports newspaper will again be of interest to a much wider public than parents and friends. Good advertising revenue will cover all the costs of the printing and many local sports stars will often be only too pleased to contribute an article.

**A Gala or a Toy, Book and Record Fayre**   A Saturday set aside in the school calendar for such a function can become a major event within the neighbourhood, but be sure to cover expenses by the sale of programmes before the day. Rain can ruin profits.

**Sale of Goods**   A friendly, hard-working art and craft department is worth cultivating, for the staff can be a source of souvenir mugs from the pottery section, key rings or wall posters. All can be made in the school and can be sold there or in any shops of parents or on a stall at the local gala.

**A Representative Match**   A special match between a local side and a team of star players, played at the local rugby club on a Sunday afternoon, can often be a crowd-puller. A good souvenir programme with a lot of advertising can again be profitable. Be careful to allow for the players' expenses which unfortunately can sometimes be high.

**Vending-machines**   By placing a drinks vending-machine or a chocolate-bar dispenser in a school, a ready source of income at break and lunch hour will soon emerge. The machines need daily filling and weekly cleaning, and the profits have to be banked.

**Broadening Horizons**

Regular fund-raising has also an important benefit in that it provides the opportunity for young players, teachers and parents to work together in a common venture—the promotion of rugby. When this sense of purpose has been created the game can be said to be truly established. But once harmony on and off the field has been achieved, the coach cannot relax for he should always be keen to extend the horizons of the boys. Success within the local area is most pleasing, but the continual restriction of matches to one area is self-defeating in a boy's and a team's development. Even the junior sides should be encouraged to travel on a weekend, or longer, tour to other parts of the country where the boys can see a different way of life and face different styles and attitudes in rugby. A mini tour for the youngest will evoke tremendous enthusiasm for the game and especially for the school. The cost of such a venture is expensive and this is where fund-raising is really an advantage. However, if the opponents are willing to invite their opposite numbers to stay with them this can ease the financial burden.

After undertaking relatively modest tours it is worth considering trips further afield. It is not being over-ambitious to think of taking teams to France, South America, Canada or Australia. Do not be put off by the scale of organization needed to arrange such a tour, nor by the cost. Think positively! If you are really determined, then the challenge is there to succeed and this will carry you through any setbacks. As I have outlined above, there are many ways of raising the necessary funds. Travel to these far-away places will fire the boys' imagination and also encourage them to devise other ways of finding the money.

Foreign tours are a stimulating experience for both the players and coach. They offer the all too rare opportunity to see how the game is played and organized in other countries. The exchange of ideas will ensure that modern rugby develops as an exhilarating game, exciting to play, entertaining to watch, with an atmosphere off the field rarely matched in other team games.